I0069171

How to Start a Food Business with Little or No Money Down

...And how to stay in business as long as you want.

Written by Annette Washington-Goff, Renton, Washington

The FoodiePreneur Press, Renton, Washington

© *2012 The FoodiePreneur, Renton, Washington*

Dedicated to my son, Derrick, who was raised in the food business. For enduring many early mornings and late nights; for spending the holidays living on the condiments in our home refrigerator because we forgot to bring food from the restaurant; for filling in as an employee when someone didn't show up; for all of the days I forgot to pick you up from daycare, and school, and football practice. You stuck with me and grew up to make me proud.

It was all worthwhile.

Thank you for being a great son.

Preface

In talking about starting a food business with little or no money down, I will show you how to start a food business with no initial cash for the space, the utilities, and the equipment. You will still need to provide the money for the inventory if your business requires it.

I will began by talking about brick and mortar type businesses where an equipped restaurant space is available and then I will touch on other food-related service businesses that have less start-up requirements.

Keep in mind that none of this will work if you do not follow a plan that gets you going from the beginning and the willingness to keep going in order to be successful. What I am describing is called *Bootstrapping* and you have to be on top of things in order to make it work. But **it does work-** I have opened several food businesses over the years using the techniques that I describe in this book.

"It takes courage to pull yourself to places that you have never been before, to test your limits, to break through barriers. And the day came when the risk it took to remain tight inside the bud was more painful than the risk it took to blossom."

—Anaïs N

Table of Contents

Introduction

"You will never get out of pot or pan anything fundamentally better than what went into it. Cooking is not alchemy;
there is no magic in the pot."

'Dishes & Beverages of the Old South'
Martha McCulloch-Williams (1913)

Making the decision to start your own business is an important step in controlling your income and your lifestyle. The first thing that you must do is to decide what kind of business you want and then you must make a plan that will get you where you want to be. Using the techniques in this book, you will learn how to make a plan, where to start searching for food business opportunities, what to look for, and what to do once you've found an opportunity.

Once you've got your plan together, you've found a food business opportunity, and you've taken the steps to acquire the business, working your plan is the most important next step. How do you keep your business going? What do I do now?

Staying in business and making a profit will be the next order of business. My main objective for this book is that you will:

- be equipped with everything that you will need to start a successful food-related business.
- be able to locate a food business opportunity, acquire it and be able to hit the ground running making money in that business.
- continue to successfully operate your business for as long as you want.

Equally important, I will show you how to successfully market your business to keep a steady flow of customers. You will have access to examples and scenarios to give you a better idea of how it works. Then, at the end of this book, I'll show you where you could go to continue learning.

In The Beginning

"The only thing to do with good advice is pass it on;
it is never of any use to oneself. "

-Oscar Wilde

How I discovered the secret of acquiring food businesses with no money down

Somehow, I always knew that I would be an entrepreneur. I was never quite like all the other kids my age. Growing up, I held several jobs at one time; I liked working and discovered early in my life that the food business was the career I wanted for the rest of my life. As a child, I grew up on military bases and after three years of college and six years in the military as a food service sergeant, I decided that I did not want to work for anyone. I just wasn't good at taking orders; I was good at giving orders, but not so good at taking them.

A few years and a marriage later, my husband and I were relocated to Fort Benning, Georgia. It was during a time when the economy was not so great and the living wage was very low.

7

One day, as I was looking through the help wanted ads, I saw a business opportunity section..., And there it was, an ad for catering truck. I thought that was an excellent idea. I could sell food and move around from place to place wherever there were customers.

The problem was that they were asking for $5,000 for this truck; money that I did not have. I thought to myself, "*I wonder if I could rent this truck until it was sold.*" I contacted the owner, who lived about half an hour away, and asked if he would consider renting his truck. I don't know how long the ad was in the paper but it must have been there for a while because he immediately said yes. I did not even give him a down payment. I sent him a payment 30 days after I acquired the truck. I operated a successful mobile food truck business which started with no money down.

A year later, turmoil turned my life upside down and I found myself divorced and all alone with a 15 month old baby in tow. I rented space in a flea market and opened my first food stand named Derrick's Café (named after my son).

 I enjoyed operating the stand so much that I decided that I should open a small sandwich shop. I scanned the newspaper once again looking for restaurants for sale. I found an ad for a café inside of a six story office building.

The owner was asking $18,000 for his restaurant. So I met with him even though I knew I did not have the money to purchase it. I thought I would be able to negotiate with the owner. When I met with the seller, we sat down and talked about what I would be buying for $18,000. I soon discovered that the seller did not own most of the equipment –he owned the toaster and the cash register; but that was about all.

When I asked the seller to tell me what I was buying for $18,000, he said I would be buying the name and the current client base. I looked around and there were no customers, no sign of life whatsoever. Granted it was in the afternoon, after lunch, and he closed at 2 PM. For the $18,000 price tag, I expected to see some sign of life suggesting that he had a booming business. At that point, I knew that I would have to do some research.

I could tell that the business was not doing well. There are always signs of how good or bad a business is doing if you just look for them. I watched the business for several days and still do not see enough business to warrant the $18,000 asking price. I told the seller that I did not want to buy the restaurant because there was not enough business during the days that I spent scouting; it did not appear to be worth the $18,000 asking price.

A few days later, I contacted the building manager and asked if the restaurant space would be coming available soon. I told him that I had extensive experience in the food service business and I was interested in leasing it. The building manager said that the current tenant was moving out and it would be available at the end of the month. I arranged a meeting with the building manager and we negotiated the terms. I agreed to lease the space and the terms were that I would rent the space for only 7% of my net sales. Talk about being in the right place at the right time!

The building manager said he just wanted to provide an eating place for the building's tenants. But I paid no money down. All I had to do was bring people (employees) and food.

After the first year in business, I added two off-premise sites at another company. I approached them because I noticed that they did not have a cafeteria inside the company or on its premises. There were vending machines, but the business offered no other food options.

I arranged to come in before lunchtime, set up tables, set up the food buffet style, and I sold hot meals to the employees. They liked it so much that I was encouraged to open a second site for the company at another location.

After some time, I began to see a pattern. Prior to getting the restaurant space in the office building, I had already started and operated several small food businesses inside indoor and outdoor flea markets. I found that I could open any food business without spending a dime of my own money to get the space. I continued to test this system in different cities in different states. I found that it worked in every instance.

During my years as a food business owner, I have spoken to several would-be food business owners. They ask how I did it. They want to know how they can do it to. After repeating the system to those who asked, I started thinking that even if they did try (and most did not); they would still need to know how to stay in business and how to make it successful. Because without this knowledge they would be out of business as fast as they got into it.

You don't need loads of money to start a business. The process for attaining a business without startup funding is absolutely possible. But the process for staying in business involves putting into play a set of systems. In this book, I will show you how to get your business with as little of your own money as possible. Then I will tell you what you must do to stay in business, stay relevant, and increase your profits year after year.

Chapter One

Cleaning House

Learn How To

- Build Your Self-Confidence

- Overcome Your Fears

- Do What it Takes to Start

Chuck the Excuses

"You should know this: you gotta be willin' to work for that American dream-work for it, and feel the passion. You gotta truly be in love with what you do. If you have a wild hair to fly a circus trapeze, to chug out to sea on a tug, to own a restaurant when you haven't much more than a dime to your name..,go for it."

-Excerpt from Paula Deen's *"It Ain't All About the Cookin"*
Paula Dean (2009)

Before we can begin, as with any life altering decision, we have to remove negative thoughts and highly contagious excuses. Many people believe that their life situations (whether it is health, education, or age) will keep them from achieving their dreams.

Top that with negative surroundings and you have the perfect recipe for distraction (or destruction) before you've even begun. You've thought about opening your own food business for many years. But as usual, life gets in the way. You've had job changes, kids, perhaps going back to school, and many of the other obstacles that have prevented you from achieving your goals.

This is the story for many people who have the desire to start their own business. Many people feel that this is not the right time, or, I don't have the money, or, I don't know where to start. Some people do surpass this point and reach the next phase, but, all too often I hear "I don't want to waste my time if this is not going to work." This kind of thinking yields a negative power that says you are subconsciously planning to fail before you've even begun.

This midpoint crisis tells me that you are straddling the fence as to whether you really want to get started as a food entrepreneur. This sort of wavering is the cause of many startup failures. Is this you? Have you made up your mind that you really want to start a business?

How serious are you? Because you can't say" I don't want to waste my time" or "I don't think that it will work;" you would be right-it's not going to work-**no matter what you do-Your mind set is what controls your business.**

Take a look at some likely reasons that you wouldn't begin to pursue your dream of being self-employed:

Reason #1
Fear of the Unknown

Are you ready to move from being an employee to having no boss, no one to answer to except yourself and your customers? What if the bills don't get paid? What will your husband, wife, or friends think? Most people will tell you that it is not a smart idea to start a business in this economy. You have to be willing to take the step regardless of what you hear. Many successful businesses have been started during recessions. This is why you need to do your homework and make a plan that will move you through to success.

Reason # 2
Lack of Self Confidence

Can you really have a successful business on your own? Maybe you feel that you don't know enough about business. Perhaps people have told you that you would never make it as an entrepreneur – and you believe them. The key here is to change your mind set.

If you are already unemployed, you need to stop thinking like an employee who is out of a job and start thinking like a self-

employed person who can make the money needed to live the kind of life that he/she desires. If you are still employed, you will have to change your mind set about how you work. Start thinking as if you are a freelancer and this is one of your jobs.

Start thinking of other ways that you can make money. This works especially well if you are planning to start a business in the same field.

Start looking at the clients that you work with. Learn how they think, how they see things. Take a look at the company you work for and list the changes that you would implement if it were in charge of this company. Putting yourself in the position of CEO in your mind will not only make you a better employee, but will also increase the chances of your success as a business owner when you leave to start your own company; especially if you plan to work in the same field. Start looking at the clients that you work with.

Learn how they think, how they see things. Take a look at the company you work for and list the changes that you would implement if it were your company. Putting yourself in the position of CEO in your mind will not only make you a better employee, but will also increase the chances of your success as a business owner when you leave to start your own company.

Reason #3
Fear of Success which Results in Self Sabotage

Perhaps you have tried to start a business in the past and either the business failed or just never quite made it out of the gate for one reason or another. Conquering fear is more than just repeating affirmations.

If you can remember that **confidence is an acquired trait that is developed over time**, you can begin to destroy the fear that you have with starting your own business or with anything you do in your life. Understand that your fear is real and that **taking action is the cure for fear**. Taking the leap and moving forward keeps you too busy to cloud your mind with the fear of not making it or not pleasing someone.

Whatever the mind of man can conceive and believe, it can achieve. Thoughts are things! And powerful things at that, when mixed with definiteness of purpose, and burning desire, can be translated into riches.
– Napoleon Hill

The Start-up Phase

In the startup phase, there are certain behaviors that you will need to assume before you begin:

- You must be absolutely sure that starting a business is what you want to do.
- You must be focused on the project at hand.
- You must be willing to do what it takes to get your business started.
- You must follow through to make your business successful.

I am going to give you some strategies that will help you to develop these behaviors. If you deploy these strategies before you start, you will be well on your way to operating a successful food business.

Strategy #1

Make a Serious Commitment

The first strategy is to make a serious commitment. Wavering won't get you anywhere. It's a simple strategy that says," ***You need to make a decision – either you want to start and operate a successful business or you don't.*** " Making this decision at this stage helps to move you through the other strategies easily.

Strategy #2

Assess Your Skills

The second strategy involves taking inventory. Writing down a list of your skills can give you a better idea of what you are capable of doing. A SWOT (strengths, weaknesses, opportunities, and threats) assessment can paint a portrait of your strengths and weaknesses. It can also identify opportunities and help you to conquer threats that may arise during your mission. Getting through this stage will also help to curb your fears of your ability to take on this project because you will know what you can and cannot do. Becoming aware of what you can do will help you to design a plan which includes forming a *success team* of people that have skills in areas that you don't.

Strategy #3

Determine the Reason

In the third strategy, you determine the '*Why*'.

Why do you want to become self-employed?

Do you want to have more control of your life?

Are you out of work and think this is only option?

Put some serious thought into the real reason that you want to start a business. The answer to this question will be the building block to your business plan and lead you to your goal.

Goal setting is an important part of your overall business plan. Knowing why you want to start your business can help you reach your goals. Without the *Why* there is no reason to continue when times are hard, there is no reason to move forward when you get tired and you ask yourself "why am I doing this?"

Using the strategies will help to eliminate the fears stated above because you will know exactly what you want, where you want to go and what you need to do to get there.

Your time is limited, so don't waste it living someone else's life. Don't be trapped by dogma-which is living the results of other people's thinking. Don't let the noise of other's opinions drown out your inner voice.., and most important, have the courage to follow your heart and intuition. They somehow know what you truly want to become. Everything else is secondary."

-Steve Jobs, co-founder of Apple and Pixar

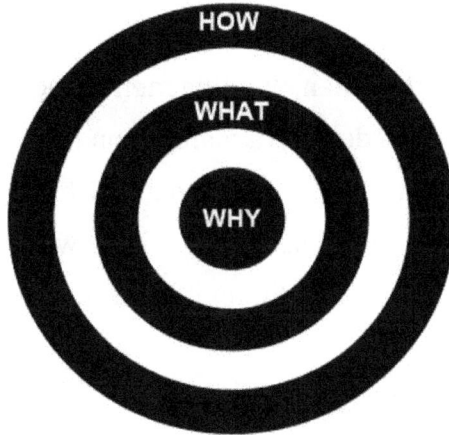

The Importance of 'WHY'

Starting with the *WHY* makes the *WHAT* and the *HOW* much easier to accomplish. If you have ever been approached by someone trying to sign you up for an MLM (Multi Level Marketing) business, you will notice that they try to sell you on the idea of financing your dreams. They ask you want in life. Do you want to pay for your kid's college? Do you want to buy a boat, or a house? They try to instill a *WHY* into your mind and then sell you on the program of choice that will get you there.

You should develop your own *WHY*; determine *HOW* you are going to get there and *WHAT* you need to do to stay there as long as you want.

Now that we've gotten all of the mental requirements out of the way, we can start to develop a plan. If you have read any materials on how to start a business, you have heard that you will need a business plan. In this section, I will show you why you need a business plan and how to use it to build your business after you open.

"I had to make my own living and my own opportunity! But I made it! Don't sit down and wait for the opportunities to come. Get up and make them! "

-Madam CJ Walker
Creator of beauty products and the first female self-made millionaire

Chapter Two

The Plan

Learn How To

- Build a Business Plan That Works
- Design Your Business Plan
- Make the First Payment on Time

"The critical ingredient is getting off your butt and doing something. It's as simple as that. A lot of people have ideas, but there are few who decide to do something about them now. Not tomorrow. Not next week. But today, the true entrepreneur is a doer, not a dreamer. "

– Nolan Bushnell

Getting Down To Business-The Plan

The concept of No Money Down is very attractive to a lot of people. Like any venture or big decision, there are some guidelines and things that you should have in place before you begin your food business. Start with a plan.

I can't tell you how many would-be business owners skip this step. A business plan is a guide that takes you from start-up through operation.

The *"it's all in my head,"* business plan is the number one plan that most people believe will get them where they want to be. The problem is that once you start working on your business, it quickly turns into a *'seat-of-the-pants'* business plan. The daily to-do list is mostly composed of tasks that are reactive to the situation at hand instead of the result of good planning. The business plan does not have to be 25 pages long. It should be a simple, easy-to-understand, vision of your business.

Your business plan is a blueprint from start-up to ongoing operation. It says what you want to do, how you want to do it and the steps you will take to get you there. You will include who will be your customer, the products and services that you will offer, a marketing plan which explains how you will sell to the customer, and your financial plan. Your business plan will also include your support team; their names and contact information. A business plan is necessary, but it is also necessary to revisit your business plan as often as needed to ensure that you are on the right track or to make necessary changes. You can also include an exit strategy that will

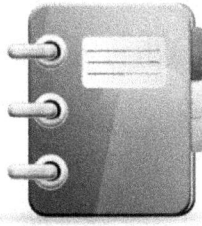

determine your steps should you decide to move on from this venture.

Sometimes it is easier to break your plan into segments. Start with your reason *WHY*, take that page (write it in big letters if you must) frame it and place it on the wall in your workspace as a reminder of why you decided to start a business in the first place. Now determine your *WHO*. Do you see a need in your community? Perhaps you already have a product that you prepare for friends and family. Maybe you know that the only neighborhood café is about to close because the owner has health issues and you that it is a vital part of the community.

Learn your target market. Find out what your potential customers want and then give it to them. It is much easier to have a customer base who will buy your product than to start with a product and try to find someone to buy it. When you find your target market, place that section of your business plan in a different folder along with the market research you performed to find them.

This folder will be used in your marketing plan. Next, you can put your financial plan together. If you know nothing about the financial part, find someone who does. This is the part when you start to build your support team. If you have someone to help you with the financial side, you will have less worries and more time to devote to the things that you do well.

Breaking up the business plan will help you keep the plan in front of you. You will be able to see how things are going at a glance.

Set milestones that reflect your goals for the business within your plan. For instance, if you want to have X amount of customers within the first six months of business, or if you want X dollar amount of sales in the first thirty days. I want to remind you that you are starting this business with as little initial funding as possible, so you will need to keep whatever promises you made for the first payment, or to make payroll. Prepare a target sheet that you can place over your office desk on the wall, in plain view.

This sheet should have your milestones clearly charted. For instance, I know that if I sell x amount of dollars of product in 30 days, I will make enough to meet my financial requirements for the first two months. Put a countdown on the sheet so that you can mark off each milestone you hit.

You should sign up for a Food Service Handlers Class. In some states, you may be required to do this anyway. It is a great learning experience and the information you receive will prove invaluable-it could save you legal trouble down the road. Write the plan that will allow you to follow your dream of business ownership. Follow through.

Chapter Three

Start with the Search

Learn How To

- Create an Opportunity
- Search For Opportunities Online
- Make the Opportunity Work For You

"The entrepreneur always searches for change, responds to it, and exploits it as an opportunity. "

– Peter F. Drucker

Conduct a Drive-by

Drive through areas that you think would be a good spot for your business. Many times your new business is right under your nose. Drive through your neighborhood and see what is available. Visit cafés and restaurants in the area.

What to look for

The type of business space that you are looking for is called Turn Key meaning that all you need to do to get started is turn the key and open the door. Look for a space that is already furnished with chairs and tables, and the equipment that you will need to start the type of business that you have in mind. Look around and try to visualize your type of business operating in that space.

If you have done your homework and made a business plan, you will know the type of business that you want to start, what type of equipment you will need, and the space requirements for your business to flow smoothly. Don't consider the space if it has too many challenges that will cost you too much money or time to overcome.

Remember, you need to be able to hit the ground running when you sign this type of *No Money Down* deal. If the business seems to have the equipment and space you need, you need to find what is happening with the business in its present state. Do some research on the area; check the businesses, schools, and demographics surrounding this potential location. Talk to neighboring businesses. If there are no neighboring businesses, you may want to re-consider this location (unless you find information that tells you this spot is going to be hot in the near future.)

Searching for an existing business or space that is vacant is one way to find your sweet spot. Another way is to visit ongoing businesses in your target area. Available restaurant space is not always advertised. Some business owners don't know that they may have the opportunity to unload their failing business onto someone else. They either don't have time to place an ad, or they are not sure that anyone would want their business, so they do not advertise it. The business could be failing for many reasons or the owner has lost the desire to continue. You should do some scouting on your own to find out more information.

Signs That a Business Is In Trouble

When a business is in trouble, the customers know it; they can feel it every time they visit. Keep your eyes open for signs that a business is in trouble. These signs are easy to spot.

For instance, when you walk into a restaurant or café and look at the candy rack or the chip rack or the beverage cooler. If you see a lot of empty spaces where product should be that's a sign that the owner could not afford to fill the rack. I know you can say that he just had a very good sales day. But, look again, check the expiration dates on the product or look for dusty products or products that just look like they've been there for quite a while.

Look for these signs that will tell you that the business is probably not doing well:

- Little or no customers at times when this type of business should be busy.
- Many menu items not available-often
- The name on the outside of the business is missing letters
- All other signage is outdated or in a state of disrepair
- Equipment, fixtures, and furnishings in need of repair

These are signs that the business is low on cash and is possibly suffering from serious financial problems or the business owner has simply lost interest. If you spend some time in the business as a customer, and you don't see very many other customers coming in; this is a sign that business is really slow. If you need further proof, visit the establishment for couple of days at different times of the day to see if your hunch is correct. You can also take note of how many employees there are. Check the attitude of the employees (if any) and the owner. Sometimes this is also a dead giveaway that something is amiss.

First, I suggest you do some research on why the business is in its present state. I know of one business where the owner had to take care of her sick husband. He had several doctors' appointments and she was the only one who could take him back and forth. There was

no one else in the family that wanted to take over the business, so she had to close.

Once you find the reason that the business is failing, list the steps that you would need to take to bring that business back up to speed. Think about your marketing plan. Could you get this business back on its feet within a few months? How would you do it? You should do your homework before you decide to take over the business.

Search Online

You can also search online for available businesses that may be willing to negotiate. You can skip the brokered business advertisements because these transactions involve a third party who is less likely to negotiate a 'no money down' situation. Websites like Craigslist, or local newspaper online editions may be good websites to search for business owners who are ready to negotiate your way. I've skimmed through the ads in my local area and have found quite a few potential businesses that I could approach with this type of offer- if I were in the market for a business.

Newspaper ads are also great mediums that you can use to find your next venture. Search the business opportunity section and look for words like **negotiable** or **must sell for health reasons,** etc.

Price reduced drastically! Must sell soon, moving out of state. For sale is an established sushi restaurant. This is a great opportunity for a Chef to own his/her own restaurant, not necessarily sushi. The restaurant is equipped for most any kind of restaurant. It has been open 4+ years with a great location that is very close to the Seattle center and the sculpture park. Owner is selling because of going through a divorce.

Craigslist gets a lot of bad publicity, but if you are careful to check every lead and remember not to sign anything sight unseen, you can find some good deals and acquire the business of your dreams. Here is an actual example that I found on Craigslist.

Of course, these tricks and tips come with caveats. When you find these types of business opportunities, they usually come with their own set of issues. It's up to you to determine whether these issues can be easily overcome or whether you should just walk away.

I will give you a few suggestions: You should always do research on the area of the business you choose.

Take a look at the neighborhood, traffic patterns, and other surrounding businesses. You can call the utility company before you sign a lease agreement to find out the average utility bill for that particular space.

Check the lease agreement for any landlord imposed limitations that may prevent you from operating your business as you wish. Be aware of some other issues that these situations may present:

Equipment Failure – be sure to check out the equipment, if it is not operable get the landlord or office manager to repair the equipment before you move in, also ask who is responsible for maintaining it. Be sure to check that all electrical outlets and switches are operational and safe.

Health Department Issues – look for signs of rodents, cockroaches, or other living creatures within your space. Check the temperatures of the refrigeration, freezers, and the hot water. I remember making donuts early one morning and being attacked by a bat.

Overall Cleanliness – in some cases, especially vacant spaces, you will more than likely have to thoroughly clean the space before you can move in. I would invite friends and relatives and have a cleaning party, just feed them and I'm sure they'll be more than happy to help.

As I stated before, once you are in, you will have to hit the ground running. Hopefully, you have completed your business plan and are now ready to get down to business. Depending on the terms of your negotiation, you will have to pay something at the end of 30 days or so.

The benefit of a business plan is that you'll know what you're doing from the start. It's not all in your head. You should get employees if necessary, get the place cleaned up and ready to open for business within a day or two. I once opened a café over the weekend – the previous owners left on Friday and I opened on Monday.

The important thing is not being afraid to take a chance. Remember, the greatest failure is to not try. Once you find something you love to do, be the best at doing it.

-Debbie Fields, Creator of Mrs. Fields Cookies

The Reason It Works

Why would anyone give you their business for no (or almost) money down? There are many reasons that this:

Scenario one

The owner is an ex-employee who worked in a corporate environment for many years and had always dreamed of opening a restaurant. The would-be food business owner quit the job or retires and uses hard-earned cash to open the restaurant. After several months, they find that owning a restaurant is a lot of hard work (I hope that you realize this as well) and that it is not generating the income that they had hoped. All of a sudden, after only a few short months, they are in debt, exhausted, and unhappy. Most times they just want to walk away. Until you walk in and tell them that you can take over the restaurant and make monthly payments to them. You negotiate the terms and both parties are happy.

Scenario two

There is a five-story office complex, or an established business complex that you have found in your area. You see that there is a space that was previously some type of eating establishment perhaps a café or a coffee shop. The shop is no longer open, but as you peer in the window, you see that it is fully equipped. You approach the business office and ask if the space is available.

From there, you find out that the previous owner got sick and could no longer operate the business, or the previous owner decided that they did not want or could not operate the business anymore and left the business as is with the equipment in it as part of the payment to walk away. Whatever the reason the space is now available and the manager would more than likely want to lease it to keep the current tenants happy. This is the time to negotiate your entrance into the space with no money down. You dazzle the manager with your experience and your business plan (you have to sell yourself and your business plan) Bring a sample to the office, negotiate the best deal and it will be done.

Scenario three

In your favorite restaurant or café, you notice things slowing down, you hear the owner complaining, and you see the owner keeps irregular business hours (not open according to the times posted) or perhaps you know the owner is ill. The owner knows you as a regular customer, so, there is a possibility that you could acquire the business for no money down. The owner may consider owner-financing because of the relationship you have built with him/her. You could make arrangements to pay a large sum in a certain amount of time or to make monthly payments.

By now, you should have the idea of how to create an opportunity that would allow you to acquire a food business with little of none of your own money down. The opportunities presented here are just a few; you can develop your own depending on the situation at hand. You just have to seek out possibilities by keeping your eyes open and acting on these opportunities.

"The critical ingredient is getting off your butt and doing something. It's as simple as that. A lot of people have ideas. But there are few who decide to do something about them-Now, Not tomorrow, Not next week, but Today. The true entrepreneur is a doer, not a dreamer."

-Nolan Bushnell, founder of Atari & Chuck E. Cheese

Chapter Four

Putting the Concept
To Work

Learn How To

- Make Your Dream Work
- Other Food-Related Businesses
- Do What it Takes to Start

Working the Dream

When all the world is telling you 'no', tell yourself 'yes' ten times louder.
-unknown

These are just some of the opportunities that you can find if you'd like to open a retail brick and mortar type food business such as a restaurant or Café. But this no money down scenario can work in most other food-related businesses as well.

Suppose you wanted to start a food-related service business? There are many businesses that would fall under this category; a grocery delivery, restaurant delivery, or sandwich delivery business. Your collaboration skills work well in this department. Visit neighbor-

hood restaurants, cafés, and grocery stores. Speak with the owners or the manager about providing this type of service to their customers.

Design a program that will allow customers to order groceries or their dinner from the local businesses. Design a form with the restaurant or Café menu; include check boxes next to a menu item with room for any special instructions and delivery information. You'll have to do some neighborhood marketing to make this program work. If you live near an office building, you can offer lunch delivery services as well.

The list of the types of food-related businesses that you can start is extensive. It is not hard to start a business with just one product. My friend Richard started a sweet potato pie business that is booming, when Debbie Fields started, she just sold cookies. People are so busy these days they just don't have time to make any of these homemade goodies. If you have a knack for hands-on cooking or baking, you can start a product food business on a dime very easily. Let's examine a few types of food businesses that you can start with little or no capital.

Catering

Yes, you can easily start a catering business with no money down. Think about what it would take to get started. You won't even need a kitchen or any equipment to start. You can add equipment to your business as your income grows.

The secret to starting a catering business on a dime is to require at least your initial cost as a down payment from your customers. For instance,

you want to start a lunch catering service with a local office building in your area. Your service provides food for lunch meetings (or breakfast meetings).

Design a catering menu based on pre-prepared products that you can purchase from wholesale clubs like Sam's club, Costco, or even your local grocery store. Market it to the people in the office building. They will call you with their orders and the date and time needed. You require 50% down upon confirming the order and use the money to purchase the food items. Purchase the packaging (such as cater trays, napkins, forks etc.) and re-package the food items for presentation. If you have a local Cash and Carry, you can purchase only the amount of paper goods that you will need. Deliver on time and collect the rest of your payment. If you want to cook your own food, you can lease a spot in a local commercial kitchen. Of course, you will need a little more of your own capital to get the space, but you can start off catering using pre-prepared products until you build up enough cash to afford a leased space in a kitchen.

Cake Decorator/Baker

Starting a business as a cake decorator or a baker is another great business idea. Of course, you will need to have the necessary pans and at least a mixer. In some states, you can even start a bakery business write in your home.

There are about 30 states that have cottage laws in place that will allow you to prepare food items in your home as long as they do not involve hazardous foods. This includes bakery items, jams, jellies, soup mixes and other dry mixes, etc. I have provided a list of states that currently have cottage laws in place:

Arizona-http://www.azdhs.gov/phs/oeh/fses/goods/index.htm

Arkansas-
http://www.arkleg.state.ar.us/assembly/2011/2011R/Acts/Act72.pdf

Florida-
http://www.flsenate.gov/Committees/BillSummaries/2011/html/7209CM

Illinois-http://www.cityofevanston.org/cottage-food/index.php

Indiana-http://www.in.gov/isdh/24884.htm

Iowa-http://www.extension.iastate.edu/valueaddedag/page/iowa-food-entrepreneurs-resource-guide

Maine-http://extension.umaine.edu/publications/3101e/

Massachusetts-http://www.mass.gov/eohhs/provider/guidance-business/food-safety/starting-a-wholesale-food-business.html

Mississippi-http://msdh.ms.gov/msdhsite/_static/30,0,77.html

Michigan-http://michigan.gov/mdard/0,1607,7-125-50772_45851-240577--,00.html

Missouri-http://health.mo.gov/safety/foodsafety/faq.php

New Hampshire-http://www.umass.edu/nefe/

New Mexico-http://www.nmenv.state.nm.us/fod/Food_Program/HomeBasedProcessing.htm

North Carolina- http://www.ncagr.gov/fooddrug/food/homebiz.htm

Ohio-
http://www.agri.ohio.gov/foodsafety/docs/Cottage_Food_Rules_Final6-09.pdf

Oregon-
http://www.oregon.gov/ODA/FSD/program_food.shtml#Domestic_kitchens

Pennsylvania-http://www.thefoodiepreneur.com/docs/uk154_pa.pdf

South Dakota-
http://www.thefoodiepreneur.com/docs/ south_dakota_requirements.pdf

Texas-http://www.texascottagefoodlaw.com/Facts.aspx

Utah-
http://le.utah.gov/~code/TITLE04/htm/04_05_000905.htm

Vermont-
http://www.thefoodiepreneur.com/docs/foodguide_vt.pdf

Virginia-
http://www.thefoodiepreneur.com/docs/legp504_virginia.pdf

Washington-http://www.thefoodiepreneur.com/docs/5748-S.SL_washingtonstate.pdf

West Virginia-
http://www.thefoodiepreneur.com/docs/64-17laws_wv.pdf

Wisconsin-
http://www.thefoodiepreneur.com/docs/Starting-a-Small-Food-Business-in-Wisconsin.pdf

Wyoming-
http://www.thefoodiepreneur.com/docs/farmersmktandlocal_wy.pdf

If you do not live in one of these states, you can still operate a product-based food business. Look for a kitchen Incubator or a shared kitchen in your neighborhood. These health-inspected facilities are popping up all over the country. You can also try the local VFW hall, Masonic Hall, or a local church that has a health-inspected kitchen in the facility. The last option is to rent your own space. As I mentioned before, this option

> *The links on this list may change so be sure to sign up for our companion newsletter at* ***www.thefoodiepreneur.com/nomoneydown***
>
> *for updates and more information about the No Money Down concept.*

would take much more of your start-up money so it should be a last resort. If you look around, you should be able to find a suitable, inexpensive kitchen to prepare your products.

If you want to start a home-based baking business, there is an abundance of information available on the web. One good resource that I found is http://www.homebasedbaking.com this website has excellent resources and lots of other goodies.

Just a reminder if you plan to bake cakes using trademarked pans (Disney characters, cartoon characters, etc.) remember that there could be some copyright issues as these specialty pans were meant for home use only and if used for sale, you may have to pay hefty royalty fees.

Once you've decided on a product to offer, figure the cost to prepare it. Don't forget to add your own income into the calculation; unless your monthly household bills are covered by another source of income, you will need to include yourself as an employee.

After all, isn't this the why you want to start working for yourself-to get an income? It is best to include your salary in your financial plan. That way, you know how much you need to make in order for you to pay your bills- household and business. I know that this may seem *'easier said than done'*, but it can be done if you plan for it. I had to learn this lesson the hard way, believe me I have paid my share of late taxes, late rent, etc. When you're ready, make up a price sheet and stop in to see each business that you plan to place your product in. You can either set it up on consignment (where you get paid for what is sold after the sale) or charge the business for the product when you drop it off.

A word of warning: be careful not to make your business dependent on accounts receivable. Catering is a cash business and your clients often forget about the great meal that you provided after the

event is over. You do not want to turn into a bill collector so make sure that you follow your own rules: 50% down to start and the balance on the day of delivery. I advise that you should not use your own money for a catered event.

You can start your bakery business by collaborating with local service stations to provide delicious baked goods for their customers to purchase when stopping for gas. You can also provide this service to smaller neighborhood grocery stores, coffee stands, or coffee shops.

Personal Chef

If you love to cook, starting a personal chef business is one of the easiest businesses to start with very little income. Personal Chefs cook in the client's home. They either bring their own pots and pans or they use the client's. Your clients will appreciate your service because they don't have the time to cook or just hate to cook! I have had single women, couples, and professionals on my client list.

Insurance for a personal chef runs from $450 and up depending on where you live and which company you choose. You can join a professional organization that may offer better prices on insurance. Liability insurance is not a requirement for this profession, but without it you are risking yourself and your business. Think of the possibility of a fire in your client's kitchen, or in case your client claims your food made them sick. The loss could be devastating without insurance. You

could add short-term or long-term disability insurance to the policy; that will pay you in case you get sick or hurt.

Plan to spend a few dollars on marketing materials. You don't need to have a high-tech office with all of the bells and whistles when you start this business. Stick to the basics: Business Cards, Flyers, and Car magnets should be enough to start.

Purchase a luggage carrier to hold your equipment. You may have one already; or you can borrow one from a friend. Choose a light, durable carrier (you may be carrying this up many stairs). Later, you can polish your appearance by purchasing a chef's coat (I've seen coats from $15 to $200+) with your name embroidered (usually about $20 extra) on it to give you a professional appearance.

More than likely, you already own the kitchen equipment that you need for this business. Take inventory of what you already own. Make a general list of equipment that you may need for each job. Proper planning will keep your initial outlay small. If you make a set of menus for your personal chef business, you will have a better idea of what equipment you will need. I had a standard list of equipment that I keep in my carrier and I purchased extra items to replace those that I used at home. The kit could cost you up to $500 or more (depending on your choice of equipment and what you already own.) In many cases, you can use the client's cookware as well which will save any initial outlay for equipment.

These are some examples of food businesses that require cooking skills. What if you do not have cooking skills? Perhaps you just love eating or talking about food. You can still start a business that allows you to express your passion.

Let's examine a few online food-related businesses that you can start with almost no money down. If you like to write, you can benefit from starting an online business. Online businesses are pretty easy to start and do not require much capital to start. In some cases, you don't even need a website. But the work will be in the promotion of your business. Getting clients for online businesses is a challenge, but perseverance will result in a nice client list.

Food Writer

If you love to write and food is your passion you could start a business as a food writer. With little more than a PC you can start a food blog, or submit articles to newspapers or magazines about your experiences with food. It is a bit more difficult to turn this into a cash business but it can be done. Much of this income comes from advertisers, adding a donation button on your blog or website, or from affiliate links of products that you endorse.

Cookbook Author/Recipe Writer

A substantial list of special family recipes or your own recipes can turn into cash for you. Publishing a cookbook these days is easier than ever. You can self-publish and place your work on websites like Amazon, or EBay. You can also offer your cookbook on your own website. You can publish an eBook that customers can view on their mobile phones or tablets. An easy way is to place your book on self-publishing websites like Bookbaby.com, smashwords.com, or createspace.com and let them convert your e-book to the popular mobile files like .mobi and epub. You can sell your e-cookbook for as little as .99 or as much as you want. This may not seem like a whole lot, but if you think about the millions of visitors that Amazon or EBay, you can see how .99 can add up to a few hundred dollars in sales very quickly.

Cooking School

If you like teaching or working in a teaching environment, you can start a cooking school. You can operate a cooking school in your home or in your city at a community center. Share your knowledge of cooking with others or contract with local chefs and have one come in each class to teach their specialty.

This short list of food businesses is just the tip of the iceberg of food businesses that will fit into the 'little or no money down' concept. If you've got your eye on a certain type of food-related business that you

want to open, review the ideas and suggestions discussed in this book. Explore the avenues of possibilities that would allow you to start with as little of your own income as necessary; keep in mind, that you will need income to keep the business going. I have listed some great resources at the end of this book to help you get the information that you need to get started.

Take-Aways

- Build Your Self-Confidence
- Overcome Your Fears
- Do What it Takes to Start
- Create An Opportunity
- Search For Opportunities Online
- Make the Opportunities Work For You
- Make Your Dream Work

Overcome your fears about starting your business. Build your self confidence-try talking to other food business owners about what you want to do. Most will be happy to give you advice about how they over-came obstacles.

Look at things differently; find opportunities that fit your criteria for the ideal food business. Start working on yourself, and then make a plan to get started and take action. By this time, you know what you want and what you need to do to get there.

Chapter Five

Get Started

Get Started!

"Nothing Happens until Something Moves"

-Dan Kennedy, Direct Response Marketing Guru

Get Moving

Well folks, it's time to get going. If you've read the entire book this far, you should be armed with some great tools and ideas that you could use to launch your own food-related business. You should have the confidence to start thinking about the type of business you want to start, the tools you need to put things in order so that you can operate with less worry about what to do next, and the drive to keep the business going once you get your foot in the door.

Starting a food-related business with little or no money down is not a difficult task. Operating the business successfully takes proper planning; this is where your hard work pays off. There will be glitches along the way but you will be able to make the best out of the obstacles that arise because you have done a reasonable amount of planning.

Being in charge of your own income is a desirable goal that anyone can achieve. There are many people that realize that working for someone else is no guarantee of a continuous paycheck because they have no control over their income or lifestyle. If a company decides to shed expenses, if a company closes, if there are people that can change your life with just a swirl of ink on a document, you have no choice but to move on. If you are the person that determines your own income, you can determine your own income needs and design the kind of lifestyle you want.

I always say that an entrepreneur should never be broke-if you need a new car, you can just go out and make your new car happen. Design a program that will make the money that you need to purchase the new car within the time frame that you want.

Of course, this may seem easier said than done, but half of the work is done once you've made up your mind that you are going to do it. You have to drum up the drive and motivation to get what you want. In the end, you will be happily self-employed. You will be armed with the tools, suggestions, and a business plan that will put everything into perspective.

It's time now. You have put your dreams on hold for long enough. I am writing this book from my suite at Coeur d'Alene Resort in Idaho. Part of the beauty of what I do is that I can work anywhere I choose. That was one of the elements of my plan; to be able to conduct business anywhere I choose. Perhaps this is not in your plan-the point is that you can design a plan that fits your lifestyle.

The next chapter is designed to help you market your new food business. We'll talk about the steps to take in order to get the sale, how to use a marketing calendar, and some ideas on where to go to get more help or information. I have also referenced information about the companion newsletter that you can sign up for online. Our companion Newsletter, The Foodie Run, includes updates, interviews with food business owners, tips, and techniques that will help you to excel in your new food business adventure.

Chapter Six

To Market, To Market

Learn How To
- Use a Marketing Calendar
- Market Your Business
- Continue Learning

Marketing Your Business to the Right Customer

"Nobody talks about entrepreneurship as survival, but that's exactly what it is and what nurtures creative thinking. Running that first shop taught me business is not financial science; it's about trading: buying and selling."

– Anita Roddick

'*Getting the sale*'-As you know, this is the key to staying in business. The ideal food business is one that fills a need or desire. Determining the right customer for your business is an important first step that you should not skip. This step alone has half the battle of operating a successful business won.

If you did your homework as suggested in the beginning of this book, you should be ready to market your business and get the highest return on your efforts.

Use a marketing calendar for your business. A marketing calendar is a tool that will help you decide what to market, how to market it, and remember when to market what. When you do all of the planning in the beginning, you will have very little work to do in the end. You input the forms of marketing that you will use and the marketing calendar helps you to organize when to act and what process to use. You can also use this calendar to track which form of advertising works and those that you should discontinue. Tracking your marketing and advertising efforts saves you money. Why spend money on advertising that is not working for you. Cut your losses and take the money earmarked for that advertising and use it for another type that is doing the job. There are quite a few sample marketing calendars available. I use the one provided by the folks at Brandeo. It is simple to use and it is free.

You can download the Brandeo Marketing Calendar here: http://brandeo.com/2012_Marketing_Calendar_Template_Free_D ownload

You can also host your marketing calendar in the cloud using Web Marketing Calendar- http://webmarketingcalendar.com

or Marketing Calendar Office- http://marketingcalendaroffice.com/products.html#

The obvious advantage of using the cloud is that you will have your calendar available anytime and from anywhere.

The third option is to use your own calendar that you pick up from an office supply store and fill in the events on the appropriate days. You can also design your own. If you use this method, make sure you add a space to chart your results. Again, it is very important that you track your marketing programs so that you know what worked and what did not.

This practice can save you lots of money that would ordinarily be wasted on inefficient marketing techniques. To make your own calendar, use the marketing categories that you have in your marketing plan (Ads, Direct Mail, Email Marketing, Online marketing, etc.) To use your new calendar, just input all of the marketing ideas that are in your marketing plan. Then break the events down by week. For instance, let's say that you have a week celebration for Chili week, or National Ice Cream Month.

Input the marketing tools that you would use for that week-

1. Send e-mail messages to clients offering free chili lessons or offering a percentage off your a related product.

2. Twitter- announce special events for chili week

3. Place Chili Week information on Blog or website and on Facebook.

Design your plan in advance for each week of the month for the celebration then when the time arrives, you will already know what to do, where to do it, and how it will be done. At the end of the celebration, chart your results.

Adapt the examples to your own business and your marketing efforts will indeed bring profitable results. Add an area for tracking; at the end of the week, write down the results of each marketing technique that you deployed. At the end of each month of advertising, take inventory on the techniques or tools that worked and those that did not do so well. You can decide from there whether to adjust or remove that technique from your list.

You now have some great tools and the know-how to get your first food business started with little or no money down. The techniques discussed in this book will work for most any business. Once you have a little more sanity in your business, I want to remind you to keep learning. There is so much information available that it can quickly become a case of information overload. Find a few good sources of information; otherwise you could easily waste precious time scouring

the Internet for every piece of information available on how to operate your business. I know that these techniques mentioned here will work for you. Give them a try; when you do, drop me a note and let me know how it is working for you.

As I mentioned before, I have provided some links to access the websites and other materials mentioned in this book. Visit the FoodiePreneur website for articles about the food businesses, the food entrepreneurs that run them, and more tools and ideas including those mentioned in this book.

Resources

Recommended Books and Materials:

Marketing Calendars

brandeo.com/2012_Marketing_Calendar_Template_Free_Download

http://www.postcardmania.com/promotional-ideas-calendar/

Books that I found useful

Outrageous Advertising-

Bill Glazer

The Recipe Writer's Handbook-

Barbara Gibbs Ostmann and Jane L. Baker

The Magic of Thinking Big

David J Schwartz Ph.D.

Instant Income

Janet Switzer

Helpful Websites:

Sustainable Economies Law Center

www.theselc.org

They have the complete chart of cottage food laws by state.

www.homebasedbaking.com

This website is great for those planning to start a home-baking business.

The FoodiePreneur

www.thefoodiepreneur.com

Our Sponsor website contains articles and Information about starting and operating a food business. You can read about other food entrepreneurs; watch Foodiepreneur TV for ideas about marketing your food business, and more. Visit us and sign up for the weekly Foodie Run Newsletter for more information about the business of food.

Freelance Foodie Magazine

www.freelancefoodie.com

A magazine for people in the food business. Read about the successes, failures, and lifestyles of food business operators. Freelance Foodie Mag includes interviews and articles about operating your food business and more.

Visit www. Thefoodiepreneur.com/nomoneydown for updates to the links in this book